COURAGE TO SPEAK: A 30 DAY DEVOTIONAL

by

Brantley R Johnson

Copyright © 2018 by Brantley Johnson

ISBN 978-1-387-75336-9

Acknowledgments

God, thank you for the inspiration and motivation to write this.

I could not have done this without my beautiful wife Hannah and her supporting me through this process. I can't wait to support her as she is writing her own book. I also want to thank my awesome kids for all of their hugs. Gabriel, Gracie and Malachi – y'all are the best kids I could ever ask for!

Thank you also to Mom and Dad. I hope I have made you proud with this one. You guys always told me I could achieve whatever I wanted to. Well, here is Book 1.

Yes, there will be more to come.

Additional Thanks:

Cindy – My sister – Thanks for teaching me how to hurry up and get stuff done ;)

Travis Wood – Editor (Check out some of his e-books in the fiction genre)

Ross Wiseman – My Pastor – You didn't just see me as a punk kid, but as someone with potential. 11 years later, I'm doing this.

Introduction to the prayer

Let's not waste time. Here's the prayer:

> Dear God,
> Give me the words to say,
> The courage to speak
> And the anointing to move.
> In Jesus name, Amen.

Super simple.

Right?

I prayed this the first time on my way to visit some friends and it did not turn out the way I was expecting.

Our friends are Jewish and let me just say, I love them. I also love the history and dedication of the Jewish faith. After all, it's the religion and heritage Jesus was born into and practiced.

Back to our friends. I have had a ton of different opportunities to spend time with them and speak with them about what I believe.

They go to temple because they want their children to develop direction, morals and tradition. I get that, but they are so close to the presence of God and I desperately want to see God do something amazing in that family's life. I want to see them come to know Jesus as the Messiah that the Jewish community looks for and as I was preparing spiritually to go spend some time with them, I was convinced God was going to do a miracle in their presence. I was going to be a part of it and watch them come to Christ!

I believe God laid this prayer on my heart. "Give me the words to say, the courage to speak and the anointing to move." I prayed it and I prayed it some more.

No miracle in their lives.

After we were back home, I was discouraged. "God, I was sure that prayer was for that trip and nothing happened." God reassured me that prayer *was* for the trip and started reminding me of the events that happened.

I had to have a couple of really uncomfortable conversations with my 7-year-old son. Conversations about drag queens and misinformation being whispered in his ear. On that short visit, I had 2 critical moments in my son's life where I acted from a place of peace and love. And God gave me the words to say in those moments, the courage to speak them and the anointing to move forward in the actions I chose.

No, this isn't a parenting book.

But it might be.

This is a book for you, because through this prayer, if you understand the heart of it and the meaning of it -

it will look different from day to day as to how God uses it.

This prayer encompasses parenthood, marriage, dating, working, existing, churching and whatever-ing. This prayer, if prayed with yielded intent, encompasses life.

It is my goal over 30 days, to teach you on some days and encourage you on others. My goal is that you can pray this prayer with confidence and that even though you may not know what to expect, you can expect God to move through you.

This prayer will change the way you live life.

IMPORTANT NOTE: All of the scripture you read in this book was quoted from the New American Standard Bible.

DAY 1

Why do we pray?

God already knows everything and He can do whatever He wants right?

Psalm 139:1 O Lord, You have searched me and known me. 2 You know when I sit down and when I rise up;You understand my thought from afar. 3 You scrutinize my path and my lying down, And are intimately acquainted with all my ways. 4 Even before there is a word on my tongue, Behold, O Lord, You know it all.

Psalm 115:3 But our God is in the heavens; He does whatever He pleases.

Well, kind of.

He chooses to partner with His creation (us). Here is food for thought: Can you find any miracle that happens through scripture where God does a miracle without first requiring some action from people? Here are a few examples of what I'm talking about:

- Moses, lift up your staff and stretch out you hand over the Red Sea - The sea parts and they cross on dry ground. (Exodus 14)

- Joshua, march around Jericho 7 times - On the seventh time they shout and blow trumpets…The walls fall down (Joshua 6)

- Gideon get rid of people in your army - opposing army

ends up being confused and they kill each other. (Judges 7)

- Elijah to the widow, I know you only have enough supplies for one more cake, but God wants you to make me a cake first - the woman has enough supplies for many days after. (1 Kings 17)

- Naman, go wash in the Jordan 7 times - He is healed of his leprosy. (2 Kings 5)

- The waiters at a wedding, go fill the pots with water - the water was turned to wine. (John 2)

- The man at the pool of Bethesda, take up your mat - He is healed. (John 5)

- The man with the withered hand, stretch out your hand - it was healed. (Matthew 12)

- Peter, come - He walks on water with Jesus. (Matthew 14)

- The disciples after Jesus' resurrection, go into the city and wait - The Holy Spirit is sent and baptizes them. The sound of rushing wind, appearance of tongues of fire and they began speaking in other tongues, testifying of Jesus. (Acts 1-2)

See. Every time.

You might even find where God requires action out of one person for another person's miracle! Think about that! You have 2 options due to your faithful interactions with God:

    1. You receive a miracle.

2. You help someone else receive a miracle.

God absolutely can do whatever He wills, but He chooses to partner with us. When we choose to accept Jesus as our Lord, Savior and Rabbi, His Spirit comes to live inside of us. We now have direct access to the Father and we now have easier access to affect the spiritual world. It is through our actions that God unites with us and therefore moves in His will.

Check out Daniel 10. Daniel had a vision from God and wanted answers. So he started fasting and praying for understanding. Then look what happens:

Daniel 10:10 Then behold, a hand touched me and set me trembling on my hands and knees. 11 He said to me, "O Daniel, man of high esteem, understand the words that I am about to tell you and stand upright, for I have now been sent to you." And when he had spoken this word to me, I stood up trembling. 12 Then he said to me, "Do not be afraid, Daniel, for from the first day that you set your heart on understanding this and on humbling yourself before your God, your words were heard, and I have come in response to your words.

Because of his fasting and praying, God dispatched an angel with a specific message to Daniel. It is through our prayers that we open the door for God to move.

Try praying this prayer right now with the understanding that you are opening the door between heaven and earth for God to do something incredible.

Dear God,
Give me the words to say,

The courage to speak
And the anointing to move.
In Jesus name, Amen.

Now, let's start breaking this prayer apart

Section 1:
Dear God

This section is designed to give you an understanding of who you are praying to.

DAY 2

The Trinity

Genesis 1:1 In the beginning God created the heavens and the earth. 2 The earth was formless and void, and darkness was over the surface of the deep, and the Spirit of God was moving over the surface of the waters.

John 1:1 In the beginning was the Word, and the Word was with God, and the Word was God. 2 He was in the beginning with God. 3 All things came into being through Him, and apart from Him nothing came into being that has come into being.

Exodus 3:13 Then Moses said to God, "Behold, I am going to the sons of Israel, and I will say to them, 'The God of your fathers has sent me to you.' Now they may say to me, 'What is His name?' What shall I say to them?" 14 God said to Moses, "I AM WHO I AM"; and He said, "Thus you shall say to the sons of Israel, 'I AM has sent me to you.'"

The God of the universe.

I AM or YAHWEH.

He created everything.

He is one.

He is three.

This is super confusing for most. In Genesis 1:1 when you see the word "God," that word is "Elohim." It's plural.

It's plural?

Yes. Here are the three parts of the one God: Father, Son and Holy Spirit.

They are one in nature, equal in power, separate in person and submissive in duties. Best way I can describe the Trinity is through the use of an apple. *(I choose apples because I don't like too many fruits.)*

(Stop judging me.)

(Focus.)

I take the apple and cut it into 3 pieces. It is ONE apple now cut into THREE pieces. Each piece is *ALL* apple, but its not *ALL OF* the apple. Right? Take a second if you need to, to think about that idea. I'll say it one more time.

Each piece is *ALL* apple, but it's not *ALL OF* the apple.

If you wanted to get real crazy, you could put a different topping on each piece to illustrate that each piece can serve a different function while still being a part of the whole apple.

God the Father sent His Son Jesus to die on the cross and be resurrected so Jesus could give us the Holy Spirit to live inside of us. The Holy Spirit then guides us, witnesses through us and helps us move successfully while still in this dark and fallen world.

One God.

One perfectly executed plan.

> Dear God,
> Give me the words to say,
> The courage to speak
> And the anointing to move.
> In Jesus name, Amen.

DAY 3

The Father

We had lost everything.

House.

Car.

Pride.

We were now living in a friend's basement because my wife and I had no money. I was trying to find work and doing odd jobs to bring in money here and there. It was close to Christmas and I'll never forget hiding the Hot Wheels track inside of Big Lots. I found this toy track in that store for $10 and it's what I wanted to get my son for Christmas, but I didn't have the money then. I would have to wait a week because I had to finish a painting job I was working on and then I would get paid.

It was the last one they had, so I knew I had to hide it. I went to another part of the toy section that was packed with stuff and hid it behind all of the other toys so that hopefully it would be there days later when I returned.

Anxiously, excitedly, I came back a week later with ten worn out dollars in hand.

Praying, "God, please let it be there."

I began looking and found it! He received it Christmas morning in a tiny basement.

In that moment, I had given everything to make sure I gave my son the best I had. The best I had financially. The best I had emotionally. The best I had physically.

In light of who God is as our Father, my best is no comparison with Him. You may be the best father or mother in the world, but your best can't touch His best.

Jesus teaches us about who God the Father is. He calls Him Father (Matt. 11:25, John 10:30) and He says if you being evil know how to give good gifts, how much more does your Father in heaven.

Luke 11:9 "So I say to you, ask, and it will be given to you; seek, and you will find; knock, and it will be opened to you. 10 For everyone who asks, receives; and he who seeks, finds; and to him who knocks, it will be opened. 11 Now suppose one of you fathers is asked by his son for a fish; he will not give him a snake instead of a fish, will he? 12 Or if he is asked for an egg, he will not give him a scorpion, will he? 13 If you then, being evil, know how to give good gifts to your children, how much more will your heavenly Father give the Holy Spirit to those who ask Him?"

Here is another thought.

He was the Father to Adam and Eve…

Think about that for a moment. Before the fall of man, there was no sin and no death in the world. Because of them, sin and death came into the world. It was because they disobeyed the Father, darkness entered in for the first time.

If you are a parent, think about all of the times your kids have disobeyed you. Think about the worst way you have reacted.

You know what God did as a good and perfect Father?

He killed the first animal and made them clothes so they would be more comfortable (Genesis 3:21). Sure, He disciplined them, but then He set into motion the sacrifice of His own divine Son, so Light could pierce through the darkness. And His Son could deposit a Helper that lived inside of us to help us move through this dark place until one day He restores it all to Himself.

At my worst, He is The Best. At my best, He is still better.

Thank you Father for loving me and counting me as one of your beloved children.

> Dear God,
> Give me the words to say,
> The courage to speak
> And the anointing to move.
> In Jesus name, Amen.

DAY 4

The Son

Look, I know if you are reading this, you are most likely already a Christian. Please don't skip over this section assuming you know who Jesus is or you might rob yourself of something beautiful.

Starting back in Genesis with Adam and Eve, everything was created and it was seen as "good" by the Father. They walked and talked with God in the cool of the day. Then, Adam and Eve took a bite of the fruit from the only tree they were supposed to stay away from and sin entered the world. From that moment, mankind was separated from God and God actively began preparing the way to put us back in right standing with Himself. He began this relentless pursuit of walking in the cool of the day with His creation.

The only way to do that was to send His Son to be a blood sacrifice to atone for the world's sin. He would show us how to live, He was crucified, three days later rose again and then ascended to Heaven.

The following scripture, I believe, is the most beautiful passage in the Bible. You are about to read a section that refers to "the Word" and whenever you see that, it's talking about Jesus. This is a comprehensive summary of what Jesus came to do as THE Son of God.

Do not read this passage lightly. Take a second and pray with me. Then, take your time to read through this and savor every line as if you had just taken a bite of the best food you have ever tasted in your life.

Let's pray.

God, thank you for your Son Jesus. Show me how beautiful your scripture is. Lord, these aren't just words on a page, but this is the whole of Your Gospel message in reference to my life. Stir me. Love me. Change me - to reflect the love and grace you have shown me.

In Jesus name I pray. Amen

Enjoy

John 1:1 In the beginning was the Word, and the Word was with God, and the Word was God. 2 He was in the beginning with God. 3 All things came into being through Him, and apart from Him nothing came into being that has come into being. 4 In Him was life, and the life was the Light of men. 5 The Light shines in the darkness, and the darkness did not comprehend it.

6 There came a man sent from God, whose name was John. 7 He came as a witness, to testify about the Light, so that all might believe through him. 8 He was not the Light, but he came to testify about the Light.

9 There was the true Light which, coming into the world, enlightens every man. 10 He was in the world, and the world was made through Him, and the world did not know Him. 11 He came to His own, and those who were His own did not receive Him. 12 But as many as received Him, to them He gave the right to become children of God, even to those who believe in His name, 13 who were born, not of blood nor of the will of the flesh nor of the will of man, but of God.

14 And the Word became flesh, and dwelt among us, and we saw His glory, glory as of the only begotten from the Father, full of grace and truth.

Dear God,
Give me the words to say,
The courage to speak
And the anointing to move.
In Jesus name, Amen.

DAY 5

The Holy Spirit

Oh man… Where do I start? Maybe in the beginning when His Spirit hovered over the deep? Maybe when He fell upon Saul or Samson in the Old Testament. Maybe with a reference from Isaiah to the prophetic turning your heart of stone into a heart of flesh. Maybe with Jesus saying He was going to send the Spirit to be our helper.

How about I start here: I was raised in a Baptist church.

What a great church!

I certainly don't want to speak for all Baptists out there, but at least the church I was a part of, we didn't talk about the Holy Spirit.

You have heard the old saying, "Ignorance is bliss." Well it was. Then someone had to ruin my paradigm about God and introduced me to the third person of the Trinity.

It was an intriguing idea though.

You know the idea that the God of the Bible actually still is the same miraculous, awe inspiring, supernatural God. What a concept! Then I start reading scripture that references what all the Spirit did through people in the Bible and it planted a seed in me. It was a seed that developed through the course of time into "Maybe God not only still does the supernatural through the Spirit, but maybe He wants the Spirit to move through and inside of me."

He became real.

Story after story in my life.

If you have been from the camp of no Holy Spirit action, I would encourage you to simply read scripture with your eyes looking for all the times the Spirit is doing stuff. You could not have the scripture we have without Him. Furthermore, a majority of what you will be reading over the next few weeks will center around what the Holy Spirit has done and is doing.

We will end with scripture today and what you will be reading will be about the Gifts of the Spirit and the Fruit of the Spirit. It is vital that you understand a few things before you read them.

The gifts of the Spirit occur to different people at different times as necessary for the furthering of the Gospel and are to always be used in a manner that points to Jesus. If they are pointing to a show or the person using the gift, it is not of the Spirit.

Next, the Fruit of the Spirit, all of the fruit, are expected to develop inside of everyone. This is how we reflect who Jesus is.

Now let's read about the Gifts and the Fruit!

1 Corinthians 12:4 Now there are varieties of gifts, but the same Spirit. 5 And there are varieties of ministries, and the same Lord. 6 There are varieties of effects, but the same God who works all things in all persons. 7 But to each one is given the manifestation of the Spirit for the common good. 8 For to one is given the word of wisdom through the Spirit, and to another the word of knowledge according to the same Spirit; 9 to another faith by the same Spirit, and to another gifts of healing by the one Spirit, 10 and to another the effecting of miracles, and to another prophecy, and to another the distinguishing of spirits, to another various kinds of tongues, and to another the interpretation of tongues. 11 But one and the same Spirit works all these things, distributing to each one individually just as He wills.

Galatians 5:22 But the fruit of the Spirit is love, joy, peace, patience, kindness, goodness,
faithfulness, 23 gentleness, self-control; against such things there is no law.

Dear God,
Give me the words to say,
The courage to speak
And the anointing to move.
In Jesus name, Amen.

DAY 6

Employment Opportunities

Leviticus 26:1 'You shall not make for yourselves idols, nor shall you set up for yourselves an image or a sacred pillar, nor shall you place a figured stone in your land to bow down to it; for I am the Lord your God. 2 You shall keep My sabbaths and reverence My sanctuary; I am the Lord. 3 If you walk in My statutes and keep My commandments so as to carry them out, 4 then I shall give you rains in their season, so that the land will yield its produce and the trees of the field will bear their fruit. 5 Indeed, your threshing will last for you until grape gathering, and grape gathering will last until sowing time. You will thus eat your food to the full and live securely in your land. 6 I shall also grant peace in the land, so that you may lie down with no one making you tremble. I shall also eliminate harmful beasts from the land, and no sword will pass through your land. 7 But you will chase your enemies and they will fall before you by the sword; 8 five of you will chase a hundred, and a hundred of you will chase ten thousand, and your enemies will fall before you by the sword. 9 So I will turn toward you and make you fruitful and multiply you, and I will confirm My covenant with you. 10 You will eat the old supply and clear out the old because of the new. 11 Moreover, I will make My dwelling among you, and My soul will not reject you. 12 I will also walk among you and be your God, and you shall be My people.

Before I was a Pastor full-time, I managed a sales team for a very large HVAC company. I learned something very valuable when it came time to hire people. Are you ready for it?

Lots of people say they want to work, but they really just want the paycheck.

Mind blowing right? (Sarcasm)

And I get it. We would all love to be able to chill at home and make a bunch of money, but that's not the real world. You've got to grind to make a dime.

Man! I took good care of my employees. If you worked hard for me, I made sure you were well taken care of. Which is one of the reasons it would make me so mad to find someone trying to take advantage of the freedom they had. I constantly found people not doing what they were supposed to and stealing time.

So…

I fired them.

That's harsh, Brantley!

Yeah Yeah Yeah.

I imagine that's how God feels a lot of times, but He's way nicer about things. Go back and read through that passage. He's saying I will take care of your EVERY NEED. However, I do need you to enact a standard of living that is reflective of your love for Me. In the New Testament, you get a similar story from Jesus. "Those who DO the will of my Father are my mother and brothers." You remember that?

See, everybody wants to be a child of God, but a lot of us don't want to do the house work.

In understanding the prayer of this book, it comes with the understanding that we serve a God who is full of an abundance of good that He wants to release to us, but in this prayer is also the expectation that we are employed for His kingdom. Our employment and execution of our Kingdom job assignment comes before the "Wow, look what God did for me."

"What God did FOR ME" comes after "What God did THROUGH ME."

Don't get them out of order.

If you're ready, let's pray this together.

> Dear God,
> Give me the words to say,
> The courage to speak
> And the anointing to move.
> In Jesus name, Amen.

In these Next 3 sections of the prayer, you will see overlap in stories due to the Holy Spirit moving through His people in complex speech and actions.

Section 2:

GIVE ME THE WORDS TO SAY,

DAY 7

On Trial

Luke 12:4 "I say to you, My friends, do not be afraid of those who kill the body and after that have no more that they can do. 5 But I will warn you whom to fear: fear the One who, after He has killed, has authority to cast into hell; yes, I tell you, fear Him! 6 Are not five sparrows sold for two cents? Yet not one of them is forgotten before God. 7 Indeed, the very hairs of your head are all numbered. Do not fear; you are more valuable than many sparrows. 8 "And I say to you, everyone who confesses Me before men, the Son of Man will confess him also before the angels of God; 9 but he who denies Me before men will be denied before the angels of God. 10 And everyone who speaks a word against the Son of Man, it will be forgiven him; but he who blasphemes against the Holy Spirit, it will not be forgiven him. 11 When they bring you before the synagogues and the rulers and the authorities, do not worry about how or what you are to speak in your defense, or what *you are to say; 12 for the Holy Spirit will teach you in that very hour what you ought to say."*

Sometimes, this verse concerns me. Especially in light of terrorism in the world today. There are literally people being executed for their faith in Jesus and I occasionally wonder, "Would I have enough faith to be like them?"

Well, here is a different question: Since no-one is currently threatening my physical life for the name of Jesus, how *is* my life being threatened for the name of Jesus? Furthermore, what situations compromise my ability to reflect Him properly where I would need the Holy Spirit to teach me in that very hour the words I ought to say? How can I choose to proclaim the name of Jesus that may draw a different look or the question from a stance of perplexity and opposition to the common logic of this fallen world?

If I fail to choose to follow Jesus and trust the Holy Spirit in the minor opposition to common world logic, how could I ever stand in the face of terrorism?

As far as I can tell, every day is my training ground. Every day is chance for me to lean on the Holy Spirit a bit more. Every day is the chance for me to choose to not engage with culture. Every day I choose to fight the evil desires of my heart for the victory of my soul.

A war is being waged every day on social media, every day in movie theaters, every day at schools, every day in headphones, every day in various jobs…

it's every day.

Holy Spirit, I need you.

I need you not just to speak, but to teach me how I ought to live in response to this world and how to live in a way that bares the fruit we are commanded to bare so that we may bare the Name of our Lord in Your finality. Teach me what I ought to say when I am on trial before friends for the covering I put over my family.

Holy Spirit teach me.

Give me the words I need today, so I can stand boldly for Jesus one day.

Are you leaning in and asking the Holy Spirit to teach you?

You should.

>Dear God,
>Give me the words to say,
>The courage to speak
>And the anointing to move.
>In Jesus name, Amen.

DAY 8

Comebacks

Acts 4:1 *While Peter and John were speaking to the people, the priests and the commander of the temple guard and the Sadducees came up to them, 2 angry because they were teaching the people and announcing in Jesus the resurrection of the dead. 3 So they seized them and put them in jail until the next day (for it was already evening). 4 But many of those who had listened to the message believed, and the number of the men came to about five thousand.*

5 On the next day, their rulers, elders, and experts in the law came together in Jerusalem. 6 Annas the high priest was there, and Caiaphas, John, Alexander, and others who were members of the high priest's family. 7 After making Peter and John stand in their midst, they began to inquire, "By what power or by what name did you do this?" 8 Then Peter, filled with the Holy Spirit, replied, "Rulers of the people and elders, 9 if we are being examined today for a good deed done to a sick man—by what means this man was healed— 10 let it be known to all of you and to all the people of Israel that by the name of Jesus Christ the Nazarene whom you crucified, whom God raised from the dead, this man stands before you healthy. 11 This Jesus is the stone that was rejected by you, the builders, that has become the cornerstone. 12 And there is salvation in no one else, for there is no other name under heaven given among people by which we must be saved."

13 When they saw the boldness of Peter and John, and discovered that they were uneducated and ordinary men, they were amazed and recognized these men had been with Jesus. 14 And because they saw the man who had been healed standing with them, they had nothing to say against this.

It happens to me all the time.

You know where someone says something rude or just mean and you have nothing to say in return. Then like 5 minutes later when you are sitting there thinking about what just happened, you come up with the best comeback and you think, "Dang it. Why didn't I think to say that?"

Ok. I am about to confess my sin…but it was pretty funny in the moment.

It happened to me with this one guy who really liked the whole playful insult thing. You know once or twice is fine with me, but over and over with the jabbing I kept walking away shaking my head, not really sure what to say.

I was having a bit of a rough morning, this same guy sees me and I am wearing a black and white striped shirt. He shouts in front of a group of people, "What happened to you!? Did you just get out of jail?!"

It set me off a bit.

I found a point of weakness of his that was obvious to anyone with functioning eyes and shouted back,

"What happened to you? Did you just get out of a bad haircut?"

Shot landed.

His jaw now hang agape.

(Ok I know you are judging me. It's only because you wish you had thought of something that quickly.)

I let my anger get the best of me and was not allowing the Spirit to speak through me or allowing the Spirit to keep my mouth shut.

Peter and John though responded from the Spirit. The priests and Sadducees were brilliant, insecure leaders that were convinced they could make fools of two of God's treasured, Spirit filled weapons. However, if I remember scripture correctly, "His thoughts are higher than our thoughts." As smart as they were, they did not have the direct connection to God that Peter and John had.

The Spirit shows up inside of them on the spot and provides insight, wisdom and witty comebacks that most assuredly left their accusers and mockers with jaws that hung agape.

Verse 8: "Then Peter, filled with the Holy Spirit, replied,"

Oh Lord that this one sentence could be spoken of me in my times of sadness. I pray that it could be spoken of me in times of rejoicing, times of anger and times of confusion. Whatever the other side of this sentence says, Lord, speak it through me and allow me to reply with all the grace of your existence and wisdom of your council. Let it not be that I am filled with mere knowledge that pours out of me in any given situation, but let it be that I am overflowing from being filled with your Spirit. For your Word says "From the overflow of the heart, the mouth speaks." (Luke 6:45)

Holy Spirit, fill me again and again.

Holy Spirit, never stop pouring.

Holy Spirit, give me the words to say.

>Dear God,
>Give me the words to say,
>The courage to speak
>And the anointing to move.
>In Jesus name, Amen.

DAY 9

Pentecost

The day of Pentecost comes and it seems normal enough. Keep in mind Pentecost was a Jewish festival commanded over 1000 years prior to this day.

It was pretty set in it's tradition.

You know, prepare the food. Read about the giving of the law on tablets….Moses gets mad and kills about 3,000 people and goes back up to get a rewrite. Read from Ezekiel about rushing winds and appearances of fire. Read about Ruth's provision, marriage and conversion to God's chosen people.

Jews from all over came back to Jerusalem for this very established festival. However, there was a difference this time. Jesus told the disciples to go into the city and wait for "what the Father had promised" (Acts 1:4-5).

Acts 2:1 When the day of Pentecost had come, they were all together in one place. 2 And suddenly there came from heaven a noise like a violent rushing wind, and it filled the whole house where they were sitting. 3 And there appeared to them tongues as of fire distributing themselves,
and they rested on each one of them. 4 And they were all filled with the Holy Spirit and began to speak with other tongues, as the Spirit was giving them utterance.

5 Now there were Jews living in Jerusalem, devout men from every nation under heaven. 6 And when this sound occurred, the crowd came together, and were bewildered because each one of them was hearing them speak in his own language. 7 They were amazed and astonished, saying, "Why, are not all these who are speaking Galileans? 8 And how is it that we each hear them in our own language to which we were born? 9 Parthians and Medes and Elamites, and residents of Mesopotamia, Judea and Cappadocia, Pontus and Asia, 10 Phrygia and Pamphylia, Egypt and the districts of Libya around Cyrene, and visitors from Rome, both Jews and proselytes, 11 Cretans and Arabs—we hear them in our own tongues speaking of the mighty deeds of God." 12 And they all continued in amazement and great perplexity, saying to one another, "What does this mean?"......

37 Now when they heard this, they were pierced to the heart, and said to Peter and the rest of the apostles, "Brethren, what shall we do?" 38 Peter said to them, "Repent, and each of you be baptized in the name of Jesus Christ for the forgiveness of your sins; and you will receive the gift of the Holy Spirit. 39 For the promise is for you and your children and for all who are far off, as many as the Lord our God will call to Himself." 40 And with many other words he solemnly testified and kept on exhorting them, saying, "Be saved from this perverse generation!" 41 So then, those who had received his word were baptized; and that day there were added about three thousand souls.

What a crazy day!

Can you imagine reading about the rushing winds and the appearance of fire for years and years; then, all of a sudden you see it and hear it?! Then, people who don't speak your language start speaking your language and telling you about Jesus.

It's insane that God lines it up so perfectly. Did you notice how when Moses comes down from the mountain the first time with the law written on stone, he finds them worshipping a golden calf and kills about 3,000 people (Exodus 32:28), but when the law written on people's hearts is given for the first time, it brings to eternal life 3,000 people? When they were reading about Ruth's conversion, do you see any similarity with her being the bride welcomed into God's chosen people and on the day of pentecost the people were welcomed as a bride into God's family?

God gave them literal words on that day to spread the name of Jesus and welcome people into life and into His family.

If He was able to give them the words in foreign languages at the exact right time to spread the Gospel, He can give you the exact right words at the exact right time.

Live in confidence that He is able and willing because Jesus said "I will." (John 15:26)

Dear God,
Give me the words to say,
The courage to speak
And the anointing to move.
In Jesus name, Amen.

DAY 10

Balaam's Donkey

Numbers 22:22 But God was angry because he was going, and the angel of the Lord took his stand in the way as an adversary against him. Now he was riding on his donkey and his two servants were with him. 23 When the donkey saw the angel of the Lord standing in the way with his drawn sword in his hand, the donkey turned off from the way and went into the field; but Balaam struck the donkey to turn her back into the way. 24 Then the angel of the Lord stood in a narrow path of the vineyards, with a wall on this side and a wall on that side. 25 When the donkey saw the angel of the Lord, she pressed herself to the wall and pressed Balaam's foot against the wall, so he struck her again. 26 The angel of the Lord went further, and stood in a narrow place where there was no way to turn to the right hand or the left. 27 When the donkey saw the angel of the Lord, she lay down under Balaam; so Balaam was angry and struck the donkey with his stick. 28 And the Lord opened the mouth of the donkey, and she said to Balaam, "What have I done to you, that you have struck me these three times?" 29 Then Balaam said to the donkey, "Because you have made a mockery of me! If there had been a sword in my hand, I would have killed you by now." 30 The donkey said to Balaam, "Am I not your donkey on which you have ridden all your life to this day? Have I ever been accustomed to do so to you?" And he said, "No."

31 Then the Lord opened the eyes of Balaam, and he saw the angel of the Lord standing in the way with his drawn sword in his hand; and he bowed all the way to the ground.

I am terrible at looking for stuff. I'll ask my wife (Hannah) where something is and then attempt to follow her directions to my hunting demise. Of course I look and don't see what i'm looking for and get frustrated.

"It's not here!" I yell across the house.

Then, with all the authority of a mother who knows everything in the world that her pitiful husband does not, she marches over and in one easy move picks up exactly what I was looking for.

Dang it.

Sometimes as I reflect on the fact that there is a spiritual world that actively intersects with our physical world, I wonder how much I miss. I wish that the Lord would open my eyes. I pray that someone whose eyes have already been opened would have their mouth opened by the Lord to speak to me. Warning me of the spiritual battle ahead. Encouraging me to be aware enough of the spiritual realm to be ready to receive spiritual sight.

Oh that I could be that donkey in times of other people's spiritual blindness. The Lord opened her mouth when she was unable to speak and gave her the words to say.

Lord, give me the words to say.

When you see, begin praying that if necessary, He would open your mouth and give you the words to say.

> Dear God,
> Give me the words to say,
> The courage to speak

And the anointing to move.
In Jesus name, Amen.

DAY 11

No Weapon

In the name of Jesus, no weapon formed against you will prosper!

Isaiah 54:11 "O afflicted one, storm-tossed, and not comforted, Behold, I will set your stones in antimony, And your foundations I will lay in sapphires. 12 "Moreover, I will make your battlements of rubies, And your gates of crystal, And your entire wall of precious stones. 13 "All your sons will be taught of the Lord; And the well-being of your sons will be great. 14 "In righteousness you will be established; You will be far from oppression, for you will not fear; And from terror, for it will not come near you. 15 "If anyone fiercely assails you it will not be from Me. Whoever assails you will fall because of you. 16 "Behold, I Myself have created the smith who blows the fire of coals And brings out a weapon for its work; And I have created the destroyer to ruin. 17 "No weapon that is formed against you will prosper; And every tongue that accuses you in judgment you will condemn. This is the heritage of the servants of the Lord, And their vindication is from Me," declares the Lord.

This passage isn't just talking about physical enemies, but the spiritual enemies of your heart. There has been set into place an army ready to attack the very people of God. There is a darkness at work every day. There is temptation every day. There is an enemy we call Satan who longs to drive a wedge between you and God.

There are spiritual weapons, plans that have been created

with the specific intent of separating you from God's best. You have to be aware. On alert.

You have to understand the forces of the world are strong, but our God is stronger!

Here is the caveat:

You cannot fight the enemy if you aren't ready for the fight. You cannot go to war if you think it's just another day in your community.

It's difficult though, right? It's difficult to realize it on a daily basis when things don't seem abnormally bad. It's difficult to be ready every single day.

I totally get it.

I think we all have the tendency to fall into complacency. Right now, you've got to be ready. God uses His people to unlock the resources of Heaven in different circumstances with the authority of the name of Jesus

So be prayed up. Ask God to open your spiritual eyes so you can be ready to fight.

Ready to love in the face of hate.

Ready to stand in the face of falling.

Ready to rest in face of chaos.

Remember, God's got your back!

No weapon formed against you shall prosper!

Dear God,
Give me the words to say,
The courage to speak
And the anointing to move.
In Jesus name, Amen.

DAY 12

Conversations

1 Samuel 16:6 When they entered, he (Samuel) looked at Eliab and thought, "Surely the Lord's anointed is before Him." 7 But the Lord said to Samuel, "Do not look at his appearance or at the height of his stature, because I have rejected him; for God sees not as man sees, for man looks at the outward appearance, but the Lord looks at the heart." 8 Then Jesse called Abinadab and made him pass before Samuel. And he said, "The Lord has not chosen this one either." 9 Next Jesse made Shammah pass by. And he said, "The Lord has not chosen this one either." 10 Thus Jesse made seven of his sons pass before Samuel. But Samuel said to Jesse, "The Lord has not chosen these." 11 And Samuel said to Jesse, "Are these all the children?" And he said, "There remains yet the youngest, and behold, he is tending the sheep." Then Samuel said to Jesse, "Send and bring him; for we will not sit down until he comes here."

12 So he sent and brought him in. Now he was ruddy, with beautiful eyes and a handsome appearance. And the Lord said, "Arise, anoint him; for this is he." 13 Then Samuel took the horn of oil and anointed him in the midst of his brothers; and the Spirit of the Lord came mightily upon David from that day forward. And Samuel arose and went to Ramah.

Could you imagine hearing God that clearly in those seconds of interaction? Hearing from God a lot of times, feels like a ton of interpretation.

"Is that me thinking that or is that really God speaking it to me?"

Super difficult.

It was just a regular conversation with God though for Samuel. Here is the important part we absolutely have to understand:

We are in chapter 16 of this book.

If you read that conversation without the context of knowing this is a man who has literally spent his entire life, from childhood through several years into adulthood in dedicated pursuit of God. You might think he was just blessed to hear from God that day.

We don't know how old he is. Everyone likes to focus on David's youth while being anointed king, but can we look at Samuel's age and dedication to the Lord?

He was taught at an early age to listen for the voice of God and you know what? He got it wrong the first couple of times he heard God speak. Go back to chapter 3 and Eli has to help him understand he was hearing from God. He spent years in service to the Lord practicing talking with the Almighty. Learning what His voice sounded like. It seems like in chapter 3 he heard God audibly but in chapter 16 it doesn't look quite like that because no-one standing with him is referenced to hearing God also.

Sometimes you may be blessed enough to hear God speak audibly to you. I have different friends who have experienced this and what an incredible testimony that is. However, most of the time you will hear God speaking from His Spirit to your Spirit and you have to take time to learn what that sounds like.

Praise God we serve a speaking God! He wants to talk to you, guide you and give you the words to say. That's one of the reasons Jesus died on the cross and resurrected back to His throne, so that we could have direct access to God on a regular basis.

However, I would like to speak a word of caution to you in your zeal to speak what God has spoken to you like Samuel. Samuel took years to learn the voice of the Lord fully and move in complete confidence of what He spoke. As you pursue hearing what the Lord has to say to you, if you have something you believe God wants to speak through you to someone,

Speak it gently and humbly.

Don't use phrases like "God told me to..." or "God said..." when you are still learning His voice.

I have seen it so many times where people use those phrases out of their zeal for their pursuit of relationship with Him and they are incorrect in their messages. They say it like it is 100% fact... but those "facts" are not accurate. The result of that is people stop believing you when you say "God has a message." Then God has to find someone else to deliver that message because you have lost your influence.

I'm not saying to not speak what you believe the Lord has told you, but when you practice speaking, use phrases like, "I think God is saying..." or "I feel like God might be saying..."

Out of your humility in learning, people will respect your pursuit.

Dear God,

Give me the words to say,
The courage to speak
And the anointing to move.
In Jesus name, Amen.

DAY 13

With God

Genesis 5:12 Kenan lived seventy years, and became the father of Mahalalel. 13 Then Kenan lived eight hundred and forty years after he became the father of Mahalalel, and he had other sons and daughters. 14 So all the days of Kenan were nine hundred and ten years, and he died.

15 Mahalalel lived sixty-five years, and became the father of Jared. 16 Then Mahalalel lived eight hundred and thirty years after he became the father of Jared, and he had other sons and daughters. 17 So all the days of Mahalalel were eight hundred and ninety-five years, and he died.

18 Jared lived one hundred and sixty-two years, and became the father of Enoch.19 Then Jared lived eight hundred years after he became the father of Enoch, and he had other sons and daughters. 20 So all the days of Jared were nine hundred and sixty-two years, and he died.

21 Enoch lived sixty-five years, and became the father of Methuselah. 22 Then Enoch walked with God three hundred years after he became the father of Methuselah, and he had other sons and daughters. 23 So all the days of Enoch were three hundred and sixty-five years. 24 Enoch walked with God; and he was not, for God took him.

Five hundred fifty seven years passed since the birth of Seth.

557 years.

We don't know how long it was between when Adam stopped

walking in the cool of the garden with God and when Seth was born, but we know it was 557 years after the birth of Seth that anybody else was known to walk with God.

I started reading the lineage in chapter 5 of Genesis and all of them were the same. They were _____ years old and had a son. Then they died at age _____.

But not Enoch.

Enoch lived and had a son. THEN he walked with God! At the end of his time on earth, scripture denotes that he did not merely die, but God took him.

Oh God, I want to live life worthy of your presence. God I want to live a life that makes you want to take me. Take me for your own relationship. Take me because I have spent my life walking with you on this broken planet and you decide to take me to your home to continue hanging out.

I don't want to live life that ends the same as everyone else's. I want to live a life here that ends with the phrase "to be continued…" because I had such a close relationship with you here on earth, everyone knows that we just continued our walking up to heaven.

God, help me live. Help me pray.

Dear God,
Give me the words to say,
The courage to speak
And the anointing to move.
In Jesus name, Amen.

Section 3:
THE COURAGE TO SPEAK

DAY 14

Esther

Esther 4:10 Then Esther spoke to Hathach and ordered him to reply to Mordecai: 11 "All the king's servants and the people of the king's provinces know that for any man or woman who comes to the king to the inner court who is not summoned, he has but one law, that he be put to death, unless the king holds out to him the golden scepter so that he may live. And I have not been summoned to come to the king for these thirty days." 12 They related Esther's words to Mordecai.

13 Then Mordecai told them to reply to Esther, "Do not imagine that you in the king's palace can escape any more than all the Jews. 14 For if you remain silent at this time, relief and deliverance will arise for the Jews from another place and you and your father's house will perish. And who knows whether you have not attained royalty for such a time as this?"

15 Then Esther told them to reply to Mordecai, 16 "Go, assemble all the Jews who are found in Susa, and fast for me; do not eat or drink for three days, night or day. I and my maidens also will fast in the same way. And thus I will go in to the king, which is not according to the law; and if I perish, I perish." 17 So Mordecai went away and did just as Esther had commanded him.

Chapter 5:1 Now it came about on the third day that Esther put on her royal robes and stood in the inner court of the king's palace in front of the king's rooms, and the king was sitting on his royal throne in the throne room, opposite the entrance to the palace. 2 When the king saw Esther the queen standing in the court, she obtained favor in his sight; and the king extended to Esther the golden scepter which was in his hand. So Esther came near and touched the top of the scepter. 3 Then the king said to her, "What is troubling you, Queen Esther? And what is your request? Even to half of the kingdom it shall be given to you." 4 Esther said, "If it pleases the king, may the king and Haman come this day to the banquet that I have prepared for him."

Have you ever put yourself in a dangerous situation? I remember one time playing dodge ball with roman candles… That was pretty scary. But I had safety goggles on - so there's that.

Nothing like the danger that Esther encountered.

She knew she had to do something, but it might cost her her life. Can you imagine the pure anxiety in her stomach as she walked down the hall toward the king's court?

Then she stands there.

Knowing there is a 50/50 shot of her death.

The scepter is extended.

She made it through her first step of anxiety. Now she approaches and has to request something.

She does and ultimately her requests are granted.

Man, sometimes we encounter situations that are frankly nerve racking. I've been there. It happens.

Whatever it is.

Then you are sitting there wondering what the outcome will be if you speak or if you remain silent. Sometimes it's easier to keep your mouth shut and hope that it all just blows over.

We may need to have the courage like Esther to speak out of a sense of protection for someone else. We may need the courage to speak honestly with our kids. Maybe we need courage to speak on a social issue.

The courage to speak on injustice.

The courage to speak for someone who can't speak - at the risk of being mocked or mistreated ourselves.

Maybe we boldly and courageously come before THE King knowing that we don't deserve to be in His presence, but it is out of His great love and mercy that He allows us to kneel before His throne and He never withholds His scepter. It's the courage of knowing who our King is and that because of Jesus' sacrifice, we no longer have to fear perishing in His sight.

Live not with the hope of one day being courageous.

Live in the firm knowledge that the same Spirit who made

Esther courageously enter and speak to the king, is the same Spirit who is alive and active every day in you.

Dear God,
Give me the words to say,
The courage to speak
And the anointing to move.
In Jesus name, Amen.

DAY 15

Both Sides

2 Kings 2:7 Now fifty men of the sons of the prophets went and stood opposite them at a distance, while the two of them stood by the Jordan. 8 Elijah took his mantle and folded it together and struck the waters, and they were divided here and there, so that the two of them crossed over on dry ground.

9 When they had crossed over, Elijah said to Elisha, "Ask what I shall do for you before I am taken from you." And Elisha said, "Please, let a double portion of your spirit be upon me." 10 He said, "You have asked a hard thing. Nevertheless, if you see me when I am taken from you, it shall be so for you; but if not, it shall not be so." 11 As they were going along and talking, behold, there appeared a chariot of fire and horses of fire which separated the two of them. And Elijah went up by a whirlwind to heaven. 12 Elisha saw it and cried out, "My father, my father, the chariots of Israel and its horsemen!" And he saw Elijah no more. Then he took hold of his own clothes and tore them in two pieces. 13 He also took up the mantle of Elijah that fell from him and returned and stood by the bank of the Jordan. 14 He took the mantle of Elijah that fell from him and struck the waters and said, "Where is the Lord, the God of Elijah?" And when he also had struck the waters, they were divided here and there; and Elisha crossed over. **15** *Now when the sons of the prophets who were at Jericho opposite him saw him, they said, "The spirit of Elijah rests on Elisha." And they came to meet him and bowed themselves to the ground before him.*

My wife is the cooking genius in our house. I don't make too much that is worth having. However, I make some mean toast.

No seriously. You would want some of what I make.

I was in my kitchen making some buttered toast one morning when my wife came up behind me and started watching what I was doing. Now, normally when I am cooking something and she watches, it is met with immediate confused looks and sighs as she tries to not correct me. However, on this fateful morning, she watched in awe as to how I made my buttered toast so daggum good.

"You butter both sides of the bread?!" she exclaimed.

I responded confidently

"Darn right."

She replied, "That's why your toast always taste so good!"

My thought is when you've got a gift like butter, why are we saving it in the fridge? It needs to be given freely and enjoyed bountifully for all of its golden glory.

While the Holy Spirit should not be put on toast, it is something we should not be afraid to embrace and ask for a double portion of. Elisha sees the mighty deeds of God done through the Spirit and decides he doesn't just want a little,

He wants both sides.

He wants a double portion.

Here is the crazy part; Elisha could have done incredible stuff like Elijah and he would have kept people in awe and lived for eternity through the scriptures. He could have been satisfied with what seemed like it was more than enough for most, but Elisha wasn't satisfied with what most people were satisfied with. He had the audacity to ask for more.

Maybe I assume too much here, but I believe through our lives we need to learn to be content with whatever God places before us with the exception of one thing -

The moving of His Spirit for His glory.

I think we get satisfied keeping the Spirit in the fridge and using Him sparingly. God sent Him though to spread the Gospel and allow people to stand in awe at the one true God in a world of a bunch of little fake gods. Little things all around us to distract us, to poison us and to break us.

Let us ask with courage the Giver of good gifts for a double portion of His Spirit and see what happens next.

Maybe, just maybe, a group of people will watch you part the waters of darkness that are near you.

Dear God,
Give me the words to say,
The courage to speak
And the anointing to move.
In Jesus name, Amen.

DAY 16

Must Be In The Genes

2 Timothy 1:1 Paul, an apostle of Christ Jesus by the will of God, according to the promise of life in Christ Jesus,

2 To Timothy, my beloved son: Grace, mercy and peace from God the Father and Christ Jesus our Lord.

3 I thank God, whom I serve with a clear conscience the way my forefathers did, as I constantly remember you in my prayers night and day, 4 longing to see you, even as I recall your tears, so that I may be filled with joy. 5 For I am mindful of the sincere faith within you, which first dwelt in your grandmother Lois and your mother Eunice, and I am sure that it is in you as well. 6 For this reason I remind you to kindle afresh the gift of God which is in you through the laying on of my hands. 7 For God has not given us a spirit of timidity, but of power and love and discipline.

Isn't it interesting how people have the tendency to take after their parents? My nephew wants to be a real estate agent like his dad who is highly successful. My pastor's son wants to be a pastor. My daughter wants to be a homemaker who takes care of children.

You've seen it before right? Success breeding success. Sometimes you see failure breeding failure.

Is it really in the genes? Were we really born to be pastors, real estate agents, home makers, drug addicts, drop outs or whatever?

Paul sees something in Timothy that I think we should take note of. He sees Timothy's faith and associates it with his mother and grandmother.

Interesting.

See I don't believe Paul believes Timothy was merely born that way. Typically, at least from what I can see, anything to do with lineage, generally involves the dads in scripture. It would appear to me that Paul is giving more honor to the mother and grandmother for teaching Timothy how to have faith like they had faith.

It would seem to me, that Paul focuses in on something that was highly important to the culture.

Relationships.

Take disciples for example. Disciples would spend around fifteen years following their rabbi. They would follow him so closely some people, as a blessing would say, "May you be covered in the dust of your rabbi." It was to say, follow so closely that as he walks, the dust from his sandals would fall on you. That's what was expected of them with regards to their relationships. It was in relationships, learning from the older and wiser that people would learn how to follow God. Look at the times where you hear about different rabbis and who they discipled under to become rabbis themselves.

Paul studied under Gamaliel.

When Peter and John were arrested and questioned, it was recognized that they had been with Jesus.

It is learning how to follow God by your association. It's

through your relationships. See, Paul has identified Timothy as having strong faith that he discipled from his mother and grandmother.

Not two rabbis.

This should encourage all of us for two reasons.

One, you should find people who are wiser than you, more experienced than you in the things of God and learn from them. Proverbs 1:5 says, "A wise man will hear and increase in learning, and a man of understanding will acquire wise counsel." Things like faith are spiritual muscles to develop. Develop them with someone who is stronger than you.

Two, you do not need to be a highly educated rabbi or pastor to teach people how to live like Jesus. There will always be someone who can teach you and someone for you to teach.

Be available for both.

Dear God,
Give me the words to say,
The courage to speak
And the anointing to move.
In Jesus name, Amen.

DAY 17

Forgiving Assyrians

Have you ever taken a spiritual gifts test before?

I have.

I scored highest on death and destruction.

No those aren't real gifts. I'm just saying grace and mercy were pretty low on my scores and I personally struggle with the attitude of justice in light of forgiveness. I love hero movies where the bad guy dies, the good guy lives and saves the princess.

Let's look at Jonah for a minute because I think he kind of feels the same way:

Jonah 3:1 Now the word of the Lord came to Jonah the second time, saying, 2 "Arise, go to Nineveh the great city and proclaim to it the proclamation which I am going to tell you." 3 So Jonah arose and went to Nineveh according to the word of the Lord. Now Nineveh was an exceedingly great city, a three days' walk. 4 Then Jonah began to go through the city one day's walk; and he cried out and said, "Yet forty days and Nineveh will be overthrown."

5 Then the people of Nineveh believed in God; and they called a fast and put on sackcloth from the greatest to the least of them. 6 When the word reached the king of Nineveh, he arose from his throne, laid aside his robe from him, covered himself with sackcloth and sat on the ashes. 7 He issued a proclamation and it said, "In Nineveh by the decree of the king and his nobles: Do not let man, beast, herd, or flock taste a thing. Do not let them eat or drink water. 8 But both man and beast must be covered with sackcloth; and let men call on God earnestly that each may turn from his wicked way and from the violence which is in his hands. 9 Who knows, God may turn and relent and withdraw His burning anger so that we will not perish."

10 When God saw their deeds, that they turned from their wicked way, then God relented concerning the calamity which He had declared He would bring upon them. And He did not do it.

Can we empathize a little with Jonah here or at least sympathize with him? Let's add a little perspective.

Ninevah was a huge city in the Assyrian empire and the Assyrians were known for being blood thirsty. They were known for war and at numerous times for their gruesome torturing of victims that opposed them.

Now, God says to you, "Go preach to them that they are living wrong so that I can forgive them."

My first thought is probably similar to Jonah. "Forget that, they would kill me! Those crazies need to die." I'm not saying that's how we should think. I'm just being honest here.

But here's the thing, God wanted to forgive them so much, He confronted Jonah's fear of death and illustrated God's desire to show mercy when justice was deserved.

Jonah 2:5 "Water encompassed me to the point of death. The great deep engulfed me, Weeds were wrapped around my head.

It's an interesting thought, right? We all assume based off of children's reenactments that Jonah floated there until the whale came and got him.

He was at the point of drowning.

God's message and encouragement was a living picture to Jonah: "You thought you were going to die and I saved you. I can do the same thing in Ninevah. You thought by not doing what I called you to do that I wouldn't show mercy when you turned back to me. I can do the same thing in Ninevah."

Wow. Who in your life needs your compassion more than your affirmation of justice? Maybe it's your kids. Maybe it's a friend or a boss.

Maybe.

Maybe it's you.

> Dear God,
> Give me the words to say,
> The courage to speak
> And the anointing to move.
> In Jesus name, Amen.

Section 4:

AND THE ANOINTING TO MOVE.

DAY 18

Nocturnal

Judges 6:14 The Lord looked at him (Gideon) and said, "Go in this your strength and deliver Israel from the hand of Midian. Have I not sent you?" 15 He said to Him, "O Lord, how shall I deliver Israel? Behold, my family is the least in Manasseh, and I am the youngest in my father's house."…

…25 Now on the same night the Lord said to him, "Take your father's bull and a second bull seven years old, and pull down the altar of Baal which belongs to your father, and cut down the Asherah that is beside it; 26 and build an altar to the Lord your God on the top of this stronghold in an orderly manner, and take a second bull and offer a burnt offering with the wood of the Asherah which you shall cut down." 27 Then Gideon took ten men of his servants and did as the Lord had spoken to him;

My youngest son is four years old and he is terribly afraid of the dark. I used to feel more sympathetic than I do now, because he couldn't turn the light on. But now he's taller, so when he starts saying he can't go into this room or that room because it's dark, my response to him is, "Just turn on the light."

That's how a lot of people think though as adults in their Christian walk. Come on. We've all heard it before, "There is so much darkness at my job" or "I need to leave this place because there are too many people who don't believe in God." How about, "I just can't keep working with these people" or "God wouldn't want me here."

I've said that last one.

Do you think that's how Gideon felt? His dad had an alter to Baal in the city…That's pretty bad. I think we can agree, that is a pretty dark place and here is what's crazy, Gideon had just learned how to live in the dark.

Really though, that's one of the options. Right? You just kind of deal with the darkness and learn how to move around. Eventually, you get pretty good at it even though it's not the ideal way to live.

You can live nocturnally in the spiritual world.

There is another option though.

You can turn on the light in that dark place. You can pull down the altars and place a sacrifice dedicated to God in its place. Some altars will be easy to pull down, others will be difficult and take a longer amount of time, but God's Spirit will strengthen you and embolden you, not to merely make statements about Jesus, but to make life change happen through loving like Jesus. Lighting up a room like Jesus.

With the Holy Spirit, in a place lacking peace, you will be peace. In a place lacking patience, you will be patient. In a place lacking self control, you will be self control. In a place lacking joy, you will be joy.

In a place lacking light, you will be light.

And yes, I know, there are some terrible situations that you need to get out of. Abuse and harassment are a couple of those situations. However, if it's not one of those, find someone to give you WISE council, then be honest with yourself and ask this question:

"Do I really need to leave or am I just whining cuz no one else will turn on the light?"

>
> Dear God,
> Give me the words to say,
> The courage to speak
> And the anointing to move.
> In Jesus name, Amen.

DAY 19

As For Your Donkeys

Little bit of back story: Saul (Soon to be King Saul) is helping his family with the livestock. Some of the donkeys take off and go missing, so Saul's dad sends him and one of the servants to go find them. They have the idea to visit a prophet (or "Seer") to see if the prophet can help them find the donkeys. Meanwhile, the nation has been begging God for a physical king to reign over them.

Future King Saul is about to get a whole lot more than he bargained for. It's like he goes in for one thing and comes out with a whole bunch of stuff he wasn't expecting to leave with. Like when my wife and I stop by the grocery store and she says, "I'm just gonna run in for milk." So, I wait in the car for like 35 minutes, call 911 to report a missing person and then she comes out with a shopping cart full of bags.

You know what I'm talking about.

1 Samuel 9:15 Now a day before Saul's coming, the Lord had revealed this to Samuel saying, 16 "About this time tomorrow I will send you a man from the land of Benjamin, and you shall anoint him to be prince over My people Israel; and he will deliver My people from the hand of the Philistines. For I have regarded My people, because their cry has come to Me." 17 When Samuel saw Saul, the Lord said to him, "Behold, the man of whom I spoke to you! This one shall rule over My people." 18 Then Saul approached Samuel in the gate and said, "Please tell me where the seer's house is." 19 Samuel answered Saul and said, "I am the seer. Go up before me to the high place, for you shall eat with me today; and in the morning I will let you go, and will tell you all that is on your mind. 20 As for your donkeys which were lost three days ago, do not set your mind on them, for they have been found.

I love this passage so much. It's really because of these two final verses. Here they are again

19…and in the morning I will let you go, and will tell you all that is on your mind. 20 As for your donkeys which were lost three days ago, do not set your mind on them, for they have been found.

Did you catch that?!

There is a fight for position in Saul's mind. You see God had already started working in Saul's mind about the events that would be taking place, but Saul was also trying not to catch himself daydreaming away from what his current task was - finding the donkeys. Little did Saul know, these weren't fleeting daydreaming thoughts in his head of becoming a king, they were thoughts placed there by God.

Disclaimer: Inevitably, someone may be reading this and thinking, "You don't know exactly what his thoughts were." You're right. But it says he would tell him in the morning and in the morning Samuel starts talking about Saul being king."

You see Samuel says he "will tell you all that is on your mind." The part about the donkeys is secondary and he says "do not set your mind on them." The donkeys are not what you need to be thinking about. Saul, you need to be focused on that daydream thought because in fact it isn't a mere dream, but it is a promise placed in your heart by the one and only true God.

Sometimes it's hard to hear Him though.

Sometimes we end up fighting a dream God has placed inside of so we can look for the donkeys. We try to keep ourselves grounded, but God is trying to lift us up to the next level He is ready to anoint us for.

I don't know, I might end up saying this a lot, but sometimes following God's purpose for our lives doesn't necessarily make sense in the earthly world we dwell in. But I mean, come on, we are talking about the same God who parted the sea, parted the largest river, made walls fall, cast an opposing army into confusion, turned water into wine, took a few loaves and fish and fed thousands, desires for us to give a tithe of our money so He can bless us with more. This is the same God who reconciled us to Himself and at the same time, using the same means, granted us authority to command healing, to command the darkness to flee and command lives to change. This is the same Jesus who cursed a fig tree and watched it wither so He could prove a point.

It doesn't always make sense, but I would challenge you to ask when you catch yourself dreaming of your potential:

"God, is this dream from you?"

If you think it is, pray some more. Fast until it won't go away. Dream until you can see what God has for you. Once it's confirmed, pray,

"God, anoint me to move."

Then stop looking for the donkeys and go prophesy with the prophets and "do for yourself what the occasion requires, for God is with you." (1Sam. 10:7)

Dear God,
Give me the words to say,
The courage to speak
And the anointing to move.
In Jesus name, Amen.

DAY 20

Greater Things

John 1:43 The next day He purposed to go into Galilee, and He found Philip. And Jesus said to him, "Follow Me." 44 Now Philip was from Bethsaida, of the city of Andrew and Peter. 45 Philip *found Nathanael and *said to him, "We have found Him of whom Moses in the Law and also the Prophets wrote—Jesus of Nazareth, the son of Joseph." 46 Nathanael said to him, "Can any good thing come out of Nazareth?" Philip *said to him, "Come and see." 47 Jesus saw Nathanael coming to Him, and *said of him, "Behold, an Israelite indeed, in whom there is no deceit!"48 Nathanael *said to Him, "How do You know me?" Jesus answered and said to him, "Before Philip called you, when you were under the fig tree, I saw you."49 Nathanael answered Him, "Rabbi, You are the Son of God; You are the King of Israel." 50 Jesus answered and said to him, "Because I said to you that I saw you under the fig tree, do you believe? You will see greater things than these." 51 And He *said to him, "Truly, truly, I say to you, you will see the heavens opened and the angels of God ascending and descending on the Son of Man."

In childlike wonder, eyes big, mouth open with a quick gasp as he realizes who is talking to him. Nathanael's mind was blown in about 15 seconds of knowing Jesus. He realized the only all knowing, all seeing person in all of creation was none other than God and therefore this must be the Son of God, The Messiah.

Jesus' response is one I imagine of somewhat bewilderment.

"Really? That's all it took for you to believe in me?"

Nathanael hadn't been completely jaded by the world yet. He hadn't been entrenched in his own doubts and disbeliefs. You can see where the process of his slow desensitization of his soul had begun with his remark, "Can any good thing come out of Nazareth?" However, that seed of doubt, planted by the dark and fallen world around him had not yet started taking root. His childlike wonder and belief allowed him to quickly see the Son of the Living God exercising what seemed to be unfathomable Godly knowledge but what was in all actuality such small spiritual muscle for the Creator of the Universe who spoke everything into existence. Nathanael watched similar to a small child watching a dad pick up a tree branch in awe, thinking,"Wow Daddy! How are you so strong?!"

That's all that it took for you to believe?

"You will see greater things than these."

Can we have the child like innocence to see God moving in the small things everyday? I would venture to say, if we can see Him move in these small, holding life together, just barely hanging on, resting, relaxing, small moments; greater things we will see. I believe one of the driving reasons the disciples were chosen at such a young age was because of this innocence. This state of mind prior to the culturally accepted desensitization to the Spirit of God, afforded them the opportunity to see God move in a completely different realm.

My prayer for us in this moment:

God, in the name of Jesus, please re-sensitize our eyes, our minds and our hearts, so our spirit can connect with Your

Spirit. Allow us to see into your realm where angels are ascending and descending on Your Son. Allow us to see greater things.

Dear God,
Give me the words to say,
The courage to speak
And the anointing to move.
In Jesus name, Amen.

DAY 21

Will and Power

Great, Brantley. You got me pumped a few days ago about standing against the enemy and I still messed up.

Again.

Will this struggle ever end?

Well I have good news and bad news. Yes it will end, but I don't know when. You have a couple of different camps on this topic. You have the deliverance camp that says the Holy Spirit will deliver you from your sin, from your addiction or depression or anger or whatever.

Then you have the other camp that says, it's all on you to rise above and put the safeguards in your life to help prevent falls. Put your head down and drive forward into creating new habits.

So, here is where I have found myself before: I prayed and prayed. I believed and believed that God was going to deliver me.

But it didn't happen.

So, deliverance must not work and I will struggle with this forever.

Come on. You've been there too.

So Brantley, should I pray for deliverance or to modify my

behavior?

Yes.

I see scriptural evidence for both.

2 Corinthians 10:3 For though we walk in the flesh, we do not war according to the flesh, 4 for the weapons of our warfare are not of the flesh, but divinely powerful for the destruction of fortresses.

1 John 5:4 For whatever is born of God overcomes the world; and this is the victory that has overcome the world—our faith. 5 Who is the one who overcomes the world, but he who believes that Jesus is the Son of God?

1 John 3:7 Little children, make sure no one deceives you; the one who practices righteousness is righteous, just as He is righteous;

1 Corinthians 9:27 but I discipline my body and make it my slave, so that, after I have preached to others, I myself will not be disqualified.

Those are just a few verses. You can find a bunch to support both thoughts.

Here is what I believe. I believe one day as I am praying, God will send His Spirit mightily and will deliver me from my hang ups. One day His power will destroy the strongholds in my life and I will celebrate like crazy when that happens. In the meantime, I'm called to pray and fight. I'm called to keep pushing forward and putting up the safeguards in my life. I need to know what my triggers are and try to beat my body till I make it my own. I am called to practice righteousness.

I am called to use my willpower to push through until His Power delivers me.

The prayer in this book applied here is for you to be able have the words to pray in the moment. Unite your heart with God and understand that God will continue to unite with you even when you miss the mark.

> Dear God,
> Give me the words to say,
> The courage to speak
> And the anointing to move.
> In Jesus name, Amen.

DAY 22

Muscles and Brains

Matthew 14:22 Immediately He made the disciples get into the boat and go ahead of Him to the other side, while He sent the crowds away. 23 After He had sent the crowds away, He went up on the mountain by Himself to pray; and when it was evening, He was there alone. 24 But the boat was already a long distance from the land, battered by the waves; for the wind was contrary. 25 And in the fourth watch of the night He came to them, walking on the sea. 26 When the disciples saw Him walking on the sea, they were terrified, and said, "It is a ghost!" And they cried out in fear. 27 But immediately Jesus spoke to them, saying, "Take courage, it is I; do not be afraid."

28 Peter said to Him, "Lord, if it is You, command me to come to You on the water."29 And He said, "Come!" And Peter got out of the boat, and walked on the water and came toward Jesus. 30 But seeing the wind, he became frightened, and beginning to sink, he cried out, "Lord, save me!" 31 Immediately Jesus stretched out His hand and took hold of him, and *said to him, "You of little faith, why did you doubt?"

I love working out. It's weird though.

It's weird how the body and mind work together during a workout. One of the things you figure out, if you work at it long enough is your brain is designed to stop you before you hurt yourself. There is a safeguard moment that happens when you think, "I'm done." However, it's the elite, the competitive, the best that figure out there is still more in the tank. There might be an extra rep, an extra round, an extra five minutes.

They know, there's more than what my brain is telling me I can do.

I was working biceps, doing curls. I had been through several rounds and I was tired. My muscles were about done and I got halfway through the movement when I stopped. My brain said, "That's enough" and I almost put the weight down. But then I decided to tell my arms to keep moving…

and they did.

One more rep.

Do you think that's what Peter experienced?

Standing inside the boat, his brain activates the safeguard. His brain tries to make sense of what is going on and tries to keep him alive by telling him to stay in the boat.

Then Peter overrides his brain and calls to Jesus anyway.

"Lord, if it is You, command me to come to You on the water."

……

29 And He said, "Come!"

The brain tries to convince Peter one last time that this is not a good idea, but Peter's spirit shouts at his brain, "SHUT UP! YOU HAVE NO PLACE IN THIS MOMENT!!"

His spirit tells his legs, "GO!"

He gets out of the boat and ignores all of the pleas to stay in safety....

He walks.

On the water.

God placed a brain inside of us. It's there for a multitude of reasons; one being safety. One being logic. But I think there is a fight we must have. It's fight between spirit and brain. A fight between faith and logic.

I can't tell you an exact prescription for knowing when you hear from God. I can only tell you it comes through experience. However, when you know He is speaking and calling you to a faith moment, your brain will try to keep you in safety. It's these moments when you need the extra anointing of the Holy Spirit to speak to your brain, to fight back and say, "GO!"

"I know what your brain is saying, but I say you were created for more than the natural."

Take wise council. Learn from those stronger than you.

And if you can tell it's really Jesus on the water,

Tell your brain to "SHUT UP!" and your legs to "GO!"

> Dear God,
> Give me the words to say,
> The courage to speak
> And the anointing to move.
> In Jesus name, Amen.

DAY 23

The Good Samaritan

Luke 22:25 And a lawyer stood up and put Him to the test, saying, "Teacher, what shall I do to inherit eternal life?" 26 And He said to him, "What is written in the Law? How does it read to you?" 27 And he answered, "You shall love the Lord your God with all your heart, and with all your soul, and with all your strength, and with all your mind; and your neighbor as yourself." 28 And He said to him, "You have answered correctly; do this and you will live." 29 But wishing to justify himself, he said to Jesus, "And who is my neighbor?"

30 Jesus replied and said, "A man was going down from Jerusalem to Jericho, and fell among robbers, and they stripped him and beat him, and went away leaving him half dead. 31 And by chance a priest was going down on that road, and when he saw him, he passed by on the other side. 32 Likewise a Levite also, when he came to the place and saw him, passed by on the other side. 33 But a Samaritan, who was on a journey, came upon him; and when he saw him, he felt compassion, 34 and came to him and bandaged up his wounds, pouring oil and wine on them; and he put him on his own beast, and brought him to an inn and took care of him. 35 On the next day he took out two denarii and gave them to the innkeeper and said, 'Take care of him; and whatever more you spend, when I return I will repay you.' 36 Which of these three do you think proved to be a neighbor to the man who fell into the robbers' hands?" 37 And he said, "The one who showed mercy toward him." Then Jesus said to him, "Go and do the same."

There are always people walking down the side of the road and honestly the thought of picking them up freaks me out. I don't know about you, but I have the tendency to make up these elaborate stories in my head about picking up a hitchhiker.

I see one and instantly it becomes a full on action movie where I have been hijacked and the guy has a gun to my head, but I realize he isn't wearing a seatbelt.

"DRIVE!" he shouts.

I put my foot to the floor and watch the speedometer increase. 40 - 50 - 60. This should be safe enough for me to live and fast enough for him to fly through the window when I hit something solid…..

I'm not joking. These are real thoughts that go through my head. Add on to my crazy thoughts that I am usually right on time for wherever I am trying to go, I don't have time to pick up strangers and help them.

Ain't nobody got time for that!

However, I know God has been working on me to do this. The time finally came where I was pulling up to a long traffic light and as I was slowing I passed a guy walking. Immediately I knew I was supposed to pick him up, but I passed him about 50 yards back. Now I start making deals with God - because that's what we do when we don't want to perform the task He has called us to.

Alright, If I sit here long enough that he actually catches up to me, I will see if he needs a lift.

He catches up.

Dang it.

So, I offer him a ride. It was a short trip and his girlfriend couldn't pick him up from work that afternoon. I saved him about a 3 mile walk home in the 93 degree heat. His name is Steve and he and his girlfriend don't typically go to church, but I invited him anyway.

Who knows if he will come or not. But, I had the chance to move when the Holy Spirit gave me the opportunity and anointing to do so.

It was exhilarating and awesome.

Maybe it's not giving someone a lift, but maybe it's providing a place for someone to stay. Maybe it's picking up the phone when that person calls who is always full of drama. Maybe it's picking your kid up from a bad situation that they are embarrassed about.

I don't know what it is, but today, I pray that God divinely lines up a situation for you and the Spirit anoints you to move.

> Dear God,
> Give me the words to say,
> The courage to speak
> And the anointing to move.
> In Jesus name, Amen.

DAY 24

Without Words

Acts 5:12 At the hands of the apostles many signs and wonders were taking place among the people; and they were all with one accord in Solomon's portico. 13 But none of the rest dared to associate with them; however, the people held them in high esteem. 14 And all the more believers in the Lord, multitudes of men and women, were constantly added to their number, 15 to such an extent that they even carried the sick out into the streets and laid them on cots and pallets, so that when Peter came by at least his shadow might fall on any one of them. 16 Also the people from the cities in the vicinity of Jerusalem were coming together, bringing people who were sick or afflicted with unclean spirits, and they were all being healed.

Wow, so the authority of the name of Jesus moved through Peter's shadow?!

No.

The authority of the name of Jesus moved through people's hearts that were bringing the crippled, sick and broken into the streets. Did you catch that? Go back and reread what happened.

Now, listen. I could go on for days with Scripture upon Scripture of different instances of this same type of thing occurring, but this is a devotional, not a thesis so I will focus in on this occurrence.

The faith that you just read about in the above passage is a faith that had nothing to do with Peter.

It had nothing to do with the crippled either.

That's weird huh?

Yeah, it had everything to do with the fact that the people who were carrying these broken people believed in the healing power of Jesus so much that they knew, if they could just get near someone who prayed and taught in the name of Jesus, their friend or family member would be healed. It was their action that prayed in the authority of Jesus.

I would like to offer the following thoughts/questions: Is it possible that our words are disposable in light of our actions?

Is it possible to pray without words?

We can pray for someone to get healed. Absolutely, we can. But sometimes, in the middle of your stress, in the middle of your sickness, in the middle of your brokenness it's just as powerful to move towards Jesus. Maybe it's not your affliction, but you are pained by your friend or family member's affliction.

I know a lady who has been praying for her husband's salvation for years and we are believing one day it will happen. Until that day, we need to continue to find ways to get him near some shadows. If we refer back to Mark 2, we have to continue to find ways to lower him through a ceiling to get to Jesus. So that when He sees OUR faith He will look to the man and say,

"Son, your sins are forgiven. Pick up your mat and go home."

Sometimes the movement towards Jesus is just as powerful

as a prayer to Jesus. This is why it is critical that we move. When we have not the words left, we make moves towards God. Scripture tells us, "As we draw near to God, He will draw near to us."

So raise your hands!

Clap!

Kneel!

Pray without words and watch as the all powerful God of the universe responds!

> Dear God,
> Give me the words to say,
> The courage to speak
> And the anointing to move.
> In Jesus name, Amen.

P.S. Remember Matthew 6:7-8? When praying, do not use meaningless repetition as the Gentiles do, for they suppose that they will be heard for their many words. So do not be like them; for your Father knows what you need before you ask Him.

Section 5:
IN JESUS NAME, AMEN

DAY 25

In Jesus Name

Why do we pray in Jesus name? Ok. So, I have said it before this is a devotional. There is a ton here that could be unpacked. You are about to get a super high level, broad overview so you can have a basic understanding as to why we pray in Jesus name.

John 14:8 Philip said to Him, "Lord, show us the Father, and it is enough for us." 9 Jesus said to him, "Have I been so long with you, and yet you have not come to know Me, Philip? He who has seen Me has seen the Father; how can you say, 'Show us the Father'? 10 Do you not believe that I am in the Father, and the Father is in Me? The words that I say to you I do not speak on My own initiative, but the Father abiding in Me does His works. 11 Believe Me that I am in the Father and the Father is in Me; otherwise believe because of the works themselves. 12 Truly, truly, I say to you, he who believes in Me, the works that I do, he will do also; and greater works than these he will do; because I go to the Father. 13 Whatever you ask in My name, that will I do, so that the Father may be glorified in the Son. 14 If you ask Me anything in My name, I will do it.

15 "If you love Me, you will keep My commandments.

16 I will ask the Father, and He will give you another Helper, that He may be with you forever; 17 that is the Spirit of truth, whom the world cannot receive, because it does not see Him or know Him, but you know Him because He abides with you and will be in you.

18 "I will not leave you as orphans; I will come to you. 19 After a little while the world will no longer see Me, but you will see Me; because I live, you will live also. 20 In that day you will know that I am in My Father, and you in Me, and I in you.

In order to understand praying in Jesus name, you need to understand what that phrase means apart from Jesus. If you were to go do something in a king's "name" or a teacher's "name," you were going and doing with the authority of that king or teacher. They had granted to you to speak or do on their behalf because they could not physically be there at the location you were headed to to do it themselves. So, the king or teacher would grant you the authority for you to act on their behalf. You would be acting in their "name."

Now with that though, there was an expectation that you would be accurately representing their will and desires. This is important, because you see where God, through His Son Jesus grants us access to speak and act in His authority as the King of kings, but there is an expectation attached: *15 "If you love Me, you will keep My commandments."*

Jesus is saying "You can speak and act in the authority of my name, but you need to be accurately representing my Father and Myself. You need to be accurately executing our will here on this earth as ambassadors for the Kingdom of God." In order to do this, 2 things need to happen: First, you need to keep His commandments. Second, you need the Holy Spirit to help Guide you in what God's desires and actions would be.

If you speak in Jesus name (authority) and it is not guided by the Holy Spirit and not representative of His commandments, I would not expect it to be done.

This is where most people find the rub.

"I prayed and nothing happened."

Scripture tells us, His ways are higher than our ways and His thoughts are higher than our thoughts. Sometimes what we think sounds good is not a directive in line with the will of God, but it is our best human understanding of a situation. Sometimes there are factors we don't know about a situation and what we thought were Godly intentions, were merely good intentions. Therefore, if it does not line up with His will, the King will not allow us to successfully act in His authority in that given circumstance.

However, faith is a journey, not a destination. We need to continue to do our best to listen to the guidance of the Holy Spirit and continue to pray. Just because we might have gotten it wrong here doesn't mean we will get it wrong next time. A pastor I once knew told me when I was a youth, "God is never going to be mad at you trying to follow His voice. Even if you get it wrong."

Just like a king would grant his ambassadors the freedom and ability to call on his resources in his name, our King has granted us access to his Heavenly Kingdom resources through the name of Jesus. So move forward in your prayers with confidence, knowing you are an ambassador for His Kingdom. And pray that God would give you the sensitivity to hear His Holy Spirit lead you in His will and desires so that you can move with His authority.

> Dear God,
> Give me the words to say,
> The courage to speak
> And the anointing to move.
> In Jesus name, Amen.

DAY 26

Healing

Acts 3:1 Now Peter and John were going up to the temple at the ninth hour, the hour of prayer. 2 And a man who had been lame from his mother's womb was being carried along, whom they used to set down every day at the gate of the temple which is called Beautiful, in order to beg alms of those who were entering the temple. 3 When he saw Peter and John about to go into the temple, he began asking to receive alms. 4 But Peter, along with John, fixed his gaze on him and said, "Look at us!" 5 And he began to give them his attention, expecting to receive something from them. 6 But Peter said, "I do not possess silver and gold, but what I do have I give to you: In the name of Jesus Christ the Nazarene—walk!" 7 And seizing him by the right hand, he raised him up; and immediately his feet and his ankles were strengthened. 8 With a leap he stood upright and began to walk; and he entered the temple with them, walking and leaping and praising God. 9 And all the people saw him walking and praising God; 10 and they were taking note of him as being the one who used to sit at the Beautiful Gate of the temple to beg alms, and they were filled with wonder and amazement at what had happened to him.

Wow, what a story! But how do you read that story? Did you read it and think, "That's a neat story, but that stuff doesn't happen anymore."? Maybe you read it and it excited you and strengthened your faith to believe for a miracle.

I'll be honest, I used to read it and think like the first response. I kind of had that distant faith like, "Yeah I'm sure somewhere in the world someone has received healing, but I'm not going to see anything like that."

Cessationism is the camp I came from and to put it plainly, it means we believed all of the gifts of the Spirit were done away with. However, I couldn't help but see some different stuff happening around me. I saw my wife affected by the Holy Spirit. I saw people at church affected by the Holy Spirit and it peeked my interest.

Is it possible God could still move in these gifts?

Is it possible that He still does miracles?

My wife bought me a book titled, "When Heaven Invades Earth" by Bill Johnson. I started reading it and it had a whole host of different stories of healing and people commanding healing. It talked about how we have become ambassadors to command the resources of Heaven to this Earth. It was incredible.

I don't know. 15…maybe 20 pages in, I believed it.

Well, I at least believed it enough to give it a shot. My thought process was, "Ok God. If this is legit, I'm gonna pray it and believe it in my better understanding of the fact that your Son died on the cross to give us direct access to you and your resources."

My ankle had been hurt pretty badly for about 6 weeks. Every day it hurt. I reached down and grabbed my ankle. I could feel where it hurt. I began to pray and command the ankle to heal in Jesus name. When I was done, I moved it around and stood up…and walked around.

No pain.

Woah.

One more story.

Two months later my son's ankle got hurt badly from him playing. My wife was out of town leading a short term missions trip to Haiti and I had to take the kids to church with me. Malachi had to be held the whole time and couldn't walk. I took him from church and got a wrap for his ankle. Later that afternoon I took him to his aunt's house because they were spending the night there.

The next morning, I was heading back home from the gym and his aunt called. "Brantley, I think you need to take him and have x-rays done on his ankle. He is wincing every time I touch his ankle and he is crying saying it hurts."

I pulled into my driveway feeling like, "God, I just don't think this is what you have for me today." I went inside my house, sat down and began praying for/commanding my son's ankle to heal. I said "amen" and stood up.

The phone rings.

His aunt says, "I don't know what happened, but he is running around my house pretending to be a pirate. I think he's fine."

WHAT?!

Can I be honest? My first thought was, "Maybe he was faking it."

No.

He was healed in the name of Jesus.

My wife comes home at the end of her trip and says the missionary spoke prophetically over her and I and said we would be anointed to pray for healing....

I don't know what you are holding onto that might prevent you from seeing God do miraculous stuff in your life, but you have to let go. Stop justifying your lack of faith. Let go and watch God do things that will blow your mind.

Let me leave you with one closing remark by Peter and John after the priests question what just happened in the above story.

Acts 4:19 But Peter and John answered and said to them, "Whether it is right in the sight of God to give heed to you rather than to God, you be the judge; 20 for we cannot stop speaking about what we have seen and heard."

Lord, give them stories in the name of Jesus.

Dear God,
Give me the words to say,
The courage to speak
And the anointing to move.
In Jesus name, Amen.

DAY 27

Preparations

Acts 12:1 Now about that time Herod the king laid hands on some who belonged to the church in order to mistreat them. 2 And he had James the brother of John put to death with a sword. 3 When he saw that it pleased the Jews, he proceeded to arrest Peter also. Now it was during the days of Unleavened Bread. 4 When he had seized him, he put him in prison, delivering him to four squads of soldiers to guard him, intending after the Passover to bring him out before the people. 5 So Peter was kept in the prison, but prayer for him was being made fervently by the church to God.

6 On the very night when Herod was about to bring him forward, Peter was sleeping between two soldiers, bound with two chains, and guards in front of the door were watching over the prison. 7 And behold, an angel of the Lord suddenly appeared and a light shone in the cell; and he struck Peter's side and woke him up, saying, "Get up quickly." And his chains fell off his hands. 8 And the angel said to him, "Gird yourself and put on your sandals." And he did so. And he *said to him, "Wrap your cloak around you and follow me." 9 And he went out and continued to follow, and he did not know that what was being done by the angel was real, but thought he was seeing a vision. 10 When they had passed the first and second guard, they came to the iron gate that leads into the city, which opened for them by itself; and they went out and went along one street, and immediately the angel departed from him. 11 When Peter came [f]to himself, he said, "Now I know for sure that the Lord has sent forth His angel and rescued me from the hand of Herod and from all that the

Jewish people were expecting."12 And when he realized this, he went to the house of Mary, the mother of John who was also called Mark, where many were gathered together and were praying.

If I told you we all experience the same things in life, would you believe me?

Peter's good friend James, was executed.

And it pleased the people of the city.

Put yourself there for a minute. You follow the Messiah, Jesus. You are friends with His disciples. They have been to your house and you have taken care of them on numerous occasions. James and Peter are your friends.

Now James is dead.

Mistreated. Most likely publicly.

And executed.

Now Peter has been arrested too and facing the same fate.

Tragedy and triumph. Everyone on the face of the planet will experience these two things. It may look different based on culture or socio-economic state, but we all experience them. Life as a Christ-follower is not determined by these events, but by the preparation and subsequent actions that follow these events.

We find Peter facing tragedy. His family and friends are facing tragedy. What separates them from others is their preparation and subsequent actions. They were prepared with a strong faith and dedication to the teachings of God and His Son, Jesus. When tragedy then occurred, they did not merely mourn and throw up the proverbial white flag of surrender and defeat. They used their preparations to dig in and began praying fervently. They prayed with a strength and confidence reminiscent of Shadrach, Meshach and Abed-nego's defiant message to the king. (Daniel 3:17-18)

They knew that their reactions to tragedy would determine their future. Their reactions to pain would determine their healing. Their reaction in prayer would trigger Peter's supernatural release.

Peter could have been executed had it not been for their faith in the face of fear. Their preparations before tragedy led them to actions that brought about triumph.

If you are facing tragedy at this moment, don't lose heart. Pray, read God's word and then pray some more. His Holy Spirit will comfort you in the midst of your pain.

If you are not yet facing tragedy, prepare. For it is in your preparations that you develop the strength required to face the king Herod of your world.

Dear God,
Give me the words to say,
The courage to speak
And the anointing to move.
In Jesus name, Amen.

DAY 28

Substitutes

Acts 17:22 So Paul stood in the midst of the Areopagus and said, "Men of Athens, I observe that you are very religious in all respects. 23 For while I was passing through and examining the objects of your worship, I also found an altar with this inscription, 'TO AN UNKNOWN GOD.' Therefore what you worship in ignorance, this I proclaim to you. 24 The God who made the world and all things in it, since He is Lord of heaven and earth, does not dwell in temples made with hands; 25 nor is He served by human hands, as though He needed anything, since He Himself gives to all people life and breath and all things; 26 and He made from one man every nation of mankind to live on all the face of the earth, having determined their appointed times and the boundaries of their habitation, 27 that they would seek God, if perhaps they might grope for Him and find Him, though He is not far from each one of us; 28 for in Him we live and move and exist, as even some of your own poets have said, 'For we also are His children.' 29 Being then the children of God, we ought not to think that the Divine Nature is like gold or silver or stone, an image formed by the art and thought of man.

Have you ever had a protein bar?

That's a weird question, Brantley.

Yeah, I know. Just go with me for a second.

Protein bars all have that same manufactured protein taste. You know what I'm talking about? Or maybe you drink something with aspartame in it and you can immediately taste it?

Why do we eat and drink that stuff? I don't think I have ever met anybody who really felt like the manufactured protein or aspartame taste was actually satisfying.

It's easy.

That's why.

It's easier to grab a protein bar than it is to make a meal with real protein in it. It's easier to drink something with aspartame than it is to drink something with real sugar and then have to work those calories off. We know it's a substitute and that they don't actually compare to the real thing our bodies desire,

but it's easier.

Paul finds all of the different idols throughout the city and in the Areopagus. He even finds one to an unknown god. Why though? Because deep within them they desire to have something or someone who ultimately can control what they have no ability to control. They know beyond their minds and into their souls that there is a higher power and authority at work.

But they worshipped substitutes.

In their worship, they sought for approval and control over what they felt like they could not control. If the circumstances did not work out in their favor, they must have done their worship wrong. What a deeply unsatisfying feeling.

I think we can do the same things. No we aren't worshipping

idols, but we are constantly trying to fix our sins. This is where many times I feel like we might be missing the mark. I believe, like the idols in Acts 17, we use our actions that ultimately are sin as mere substitutes for Godly things we cannot control.

If you have a problem with lust, you have replaced the genuine desire for your spouse with desire for anything that will temporarily fix the desire you have. Why? Because you cannot control the circumstances that surround your spouse wanting to be intimate and the circumstances that present themselves available at the right time for you to be intimate. Therefore, you run to something easy, even though you know it doesn't satisfy you the same way. The way God desires for you to be satisfied.

If you have a problem with gossip, you have replaced the God given desire of fellowship, relationship and emotional intimacy with quick information that may or may not be accurate so that you can feel a connection with someone you really don't have a genuine connection with. Why? Because it's quicker to feel like you are part of the conversation. It's easier than feeling left out or alone for a short time while you invest into real, God-given relationships that you aren't 100% sure on a timeline as to when they will develop into the relationships you long for.

Maybe the problem we face is not so much the sin at face value, but perhaps the sin we engage in is just a mere substitute for desires we cannot control.

We will never be able to "fix" the sin in our lives as long as we are focused on fixing the sin instead of focusing our eyes on Jesus.

Paul, please preach to me about the goodness of the ONE true God. In Jesus name, help me to desire the realness of God and not the substitutes of the easy.

Dear God,
Give me the words to say,
The courage to speak
And the anointing to move.
In Jesus name, Amen.

DAY 29

Uncomfortable

Mark 5:1 They came to the other side of the sea, into the country of the Gerasenes. 2 When He got out of the boat, immediately a man from the tombs with an unclean spirit met Him, 3 and he had his dwelling among the tombs. And no one was able to bind him anymore, even with a chain; 4 because he had often been bound with shackles and chains, and the chains had been torn apart by him and the shackles broken in pieces, and no one was strong enough to subdue him. 5 Constantly, night and day, he was screaming among the tombs and in the mountains, and gashing himself with stones. 6 Seeing Jesus from a distance, he ran up and bowed down before Him; 7 and shouting with a loud voice, he *said, "What business do we have with each other, Jesus, Son of the Most High God? I implore You by God, do not torment me!" 8 For He had been saying to him, "Come out of the man, you unclean spirit!" 9 And He was asking him, "What is your name?" And he *said to Him, "My name is Legion; for we are many." 10 And he began to implore Him earnestly not to send them out of the country. 11 Now there was a large herd of swine feeding nearby on the mountain. 12 The demons implored Him, saying, "Send us into the swine so that we may enter them." 13 Jesus gave them permission. And coming out, the unclean spirits entered the swine; and the herd rushed down the steep bank into the sea, about two thousand of them; and they were drowned in the sea.

14 Their herdsmen ran away and reported it in the city and in the country. And the people came to see what it was that had happened. 15 They *came to Jesus and *observed the man *who had been demon-possessed sitting down, clothed and in his right mind, the very man who had had the "legion"; and they became frightened. 16 Those who had seen it described to them how it had happened to the demon-possessed man, and all about the swine. 17 And they began to implore Him to leave their region.*

Many people believe it to be a random choice by Jesus to allow the demons to enter the herd of swine. However, there is more to this story. There is more of a love for people in this story than just the man delivered from the possession of the demons.

Any disciple could have done that.

Any disciple could have had the love for that man's existence, that they would choose to free him from the enslavement to demons.

Jesus though, saw the larger picture.

We need to understand Jesus was visiting the Decapolis. It was a highly pagan group of cities and their gods required sacrifice. The primary sacrifice to those gods -

pigs.

These herdsmen, are believed by some scholars to have been herding swine for the specific purpose of temple sacrifice to these pagan gods.

Jesus understands the full situation as he walks across the beach and encounters this demon possessed man. This is not just a man controlled by demons, but an entire region controlled by demons.

So, when Jesus commands the demons to come out of the man and sends them into the swine, He is not only casting demons out of the man, but as the pigs drown in the sea, He has also cast demons out of the land.

This is why we see the people begging Him to leave. What will they do without the ability to sacrifice to their gods? What will they do without the ability to do what they have always done? They were comfortable in their lives and Jesus came along to make them uncomfortable.

What happens when God chooses to invade our space? When the Holy Spirit begins casting demons out of our lives?

No. Not real demons like possession, but demons like a little alcohol, the insults, the alone time, a specific show or movie. What happens when He asks for more of your social media time so He can spend time with you?

I'll tell you what your tendency will be.

17 And they began to implore Him to leave their region.

No. You certainly would not intentionally think that, but your actions begin the process of imploring Him to leave. You have to fight it though. If Jesus shows up on the beach of your life confronting your demons, let them go.

I know.

It's easier said than done.

But, in the name of Jesus Christ the Nazarene - let them go and don't chase after them.

If Jesus is casting something from you now, pray with me.

>Dear God,
>Give me the words to say,
>The courage to speak
>And the anointing to move.
>In Jesus name, Amen.

DAY 30

Prophetic

Well, this is it. What a journey we have been on together. Take a second to thank God for His scriptures and then let's read the final devotion together.

John 11:1 Now a certain man was sick, Lazarus of Bethany, the village of Mary and her sister Martha. 2 It was the Mary who anointed the Lord with ointment, and wiped His feet with her hair, whose brother Lazarus was sick. 3 So the sisters sent word to Him, saying, "Lord, behold, he whom You love is sick." 4 But when Jesus heard this, He said, "This sickness is not to end in death, but for the glory of God, so that the Son of God may be glorified by it."…

…30 Now Jesus had not yet come into the village, but was still in the place where Martha met Him. 31 Then the Jews who were with her in the house, and consoling her, when they saw that Mary got up quickly and went out, they followed her, supposing that she was going to the tomb to weep there. 32 Therefore, when Mary came where Jesus was, she saw Him, and fell at His feet, saying to Him, "Lord, if You had been here, my brother would not have died." 33 When Jesus therefore saw her weeping, and the Jews who came with her also weeping, He was deeply moved in spirit and was troubled, 34 and said, "Where have you laid him?" They *said to Him, "Lord, come and see." 35 Jesus wept. 36 So the Jews were saying, "See how He loved him!" 37 But some of them said, "Could not this man, who opened the eyes of the blind man, have kept this man also from dying?"

38 So Jesus, again being deeply moved within, *came to the tomb. Now it was a cave, and a stone was lying against it. 39 Jesus *said, "Remove the stone." Martha, the sister of the deceased, *said to Him, "Lord, by this time there will be a stench, for he has been dead four days." 40 Jesus *said to her, "Did I not say to you that if you believe, you will see the glory of God?" 41 So they removed the stone. Then Jesus raised His eyes, and said, "Father, I thank You that You have heard Me. 42 I knew that You always hear Me; but because of the people standing around I said it, so that they may believe that You sent Me." 43 When He had said these things, He cried out with a loud voice, "Lazarus, come forth." 44 The man who had died came forth, bound hand and foot with wrappings, and his face was wrapped around with a cloth. Jesus *said to them, "Unbind him, and let him go."

I read this and see it as symbolically prophetic for us.

Prophetic for us on a few different levels.

Life is so hard. When looking at our Christian walk, it is easy to misstep. The enemy has laid traps for us all along our paths. Every day is a fight.

I hold onto what Jesus said about Lazarus though. Sometimes I think Jesus is talking directly to me when He said,

4 "This sickness is not to end in death"

This is motivation for me. We know Jesus is coming back for us. We know through Jesus' death and resurrection, God has adopted us as sons and daughters, as heirs to His kingdom.

When I feel the sickness of this world calling me to death, I am reminded that this sickness will not end in death. When I feel that I have been set in a field of traps I am reminded that "he who practices righteousness is righteous just as He is righteous." As long as I practice where to put my foot; the occasions I step into a trap, Jesus with all the authority of the all powerful God, commands my tomb to be opened up. And with passion in His voice he looks into our sickness, into our tomb, into our frailty, into our hearts and with a loud voice says, "Come Forth!"

This passage, I think is prophetic - for our time on earth and our time after our flesh expires.

This sickness we experience here on earth will not end in death. Yes, our earthly body will pass away, but then the Lord of all creation will look into our tomb with the power of eternity and will command us to come forth into His Heavenly Kingdom. He will look to His angels and order them to,

"Unbind him, and let him go."

Then we will be able to walk freely into eternity.

Hallelujah Lord!

Until that day, we have a mandate to live like Jesus lived. I want to draw your attention to one final piece. The reason for the prayer we have been walking through for 30 days is found here in what Jesus says just before He calls Lazarus out of the tomb.

41 "Father, I thank You that You have heard Me. 42 I knew that You always hear Me; but because of the people standing around I said it, so that they may believe that You sent Me."

The point of the prayer is this, that you live like Jesus because of the *people standing around you*. Here is what I think is interesting about this statement. Yes we are called to live as testimonies for those who don't believe in Jesus yet, but all the people who were standing around Jesus in that moment were already friends and followers. It's almost as if our faith needs to be restored daily in the Lord we serve.

Seems very reminiscent of the Old Testament don't you think?

Pray this with me one last time.

Dear God,
Give me the words to say,
The courage to speak
And the anointing to move.
In Jesus name, Amen.

Made in the USA
Columbia, SC
18 March 2020